The War on Idigna

The War on Idigna

Waleed Al-Bazoon

To order additional copies of this book, contact:
Xlibris Corporation
0-800-644-6988
www.XlibrisPublishing.co.uk
Orders@XlibrisPublishing.co.uk
302431

Contents

These verses are dedicated to
the souls of Iraqis that passed away in war after war,
in the international embargo on Iraq
and in the underground prisons of the despot.

Acknowledgements

My first words of gratitude are due to Mrs. Anne Lonsdale and Dr. Leo Mellor whose references helped shape my career as a researcher and a PhD candidate at the University of Chichester during the period of writing this collection. I am grateful to the council for assisting refugee academics (CARA) in London for sponsoring my study during the period of writing this collection. Special thanks to Dr John Ashworth, Professor John Akker, Professor Robin Baker, Kate Robertson, and Annalisa. Special thanks are due to the staff of the department of English and Creative Writing at the University of Chichester whose creative guidance and advice are of utmost importance to me in terms of leading me to the right way in writing creatively. I would like to express my gratitude to Dr. Hugh Denkerley who has read and revised the first draft of most of the poems included in this collection. My deepest gratitude to the following professors: Diana Barsham, Robert Dugan, Jessica De Mellow, Alison Macleod, Stephanie Norgate and David Swann who have read some of my creative writings that encouraged me later to write this collection. Special thanks to the following academic staff for their moral encouragement during my stay in the department: Professor Bill Gray, Dr. Stavroula Varella, Dr Fiona Price, Dr Ben Noys, Dr Karen Stevens, Stephen Mollet and to Lorna Sargent.

Special thanks to Brian Turner who has read some of my poems in the early stage of writing this collection. My gratitude is to John Dane, the chaplain at the University of Chichester, for his continuous cooperation and help. I wish to express special thanks for the support given to me by my friend Douglas and his wife Wendy. My gratitude is due to my friends Dr. Amir AL-Azraqi, and Dr. Muhammad Al-Maliki who have morally supported me during the writing of this collection. Special thanks to my patient family for all their time and support.

1

I want to cry with a hundred children under the sun
I want one of them to explain to me
The value of peace that equals the value of war!

Hassan Blasim

Trade Mark

My country has only one trade.
That trade has many faces.
Sometimes it imports bullets,
Other times coffins.
Mostly it exports the blood of its citizens.
The organs of their bodies.
The legs, the heads, the arms.
But their hearts are missed in this export!
These hearts are shown on flags of elections.
When the millions march slowly in the dark...
When the millions tread on the dreams of their deceased forefathers.
When the brown faces carry the dead futures of their aborted babies.
When the millions give their hearts blood to sign for the seat of power.
To those who would come to our land.
To save the infants.
To free the wishes.
To build an exploded mosque and a destroyed church.
To wash the land clean of blood.
The power seekers who said and say and keep saying that
"We are the saviours".
There is no other savior.
These millions bring all they have with them.
Their eyes, legs, arms, dreams.
Wishes, blood, and all they have.
They put them all on the golden plates of the waited for saviour,
Who tells them every morning,
That he is the god which will save them.
He is the painter of their hearts with the colours of life.
That he is the waited for saviour.
That he is the no more prisons, suffering and torture.
That he will build the church before the mosque.
And theatres before barges.
He will light their nights.
And send them all to see the moon.
The new prime minister the millions dreamt of, signed for, trod on their dreams to
    see his dream realized,

He who dreams only of himself and power.

This is my country, one trade it has and one dream still unrealized yet.

It always learns to give, learns to grant, and learns to leave its loaf for others to eat.

My country has no word in its dictionary as "take" for it knows only the language of giving.

One trade my country has, my country has.

City of Peace

At the heart of my country lies a city,
Baghdad it is called.
The ancient name it once had is "the city of peace",
Where the prayers rise from Musa AL-Kadhum's sacred shrine,
To hug the doors of heaven.
City of peace is,
Where the sermons of its churches penetrate the heart of the cross.
The city of peace, oh, no, Baghdad I am called.
And I want to show you what it means to be Baghdad.
And the B means the birth of no bloom.
And the A means that art is slaughtered.
And the G means go everywhere, oh, millions of marching people,
Go to the bleeding Tigris.
Go to the crying Euphrates.
Go to the land of prophets.
But you will find nothing but bullets, blood, and anything good for nothing.
This is what is meant by "Bag".
And the "dad" refers to the date after date,
When these millions woke up by force suddenly after 2003.
And found the Sunni and the Shiite embrace on the brink of the shore of blood.
When they kissed the blades of knives
And spat on the shaking of the hands.
The 'dad' refers and refers,
To the date after date.
To the war after war.
And the bomb after bomb that cut our veins.
And the bullet after the bullet.
The casket after the casket.
It refers to the call of peace that was killed on the gate of our mosques.
It refers to the trace of mercy that was kidnapped on the steps of our churches.
It refers to the death of the smile on the doors of nurseries.
It means the drowning of the sects in the depth of Idigna.
It means the rising of the flags of violent fingers and red hearts.
The "dad" refers and refers, so do not be appalled by its meanings.
It refers to the blossoming of grudge.
It refers to the absence of love in the land of verse and rhyme.

5

More and more…
It refers to the war on man in the land of Cain.
It refers to the soul of my dad, who was buried in the boot of a car,
In the wake of 2006.
Whose eyes were bandaged by darkness on the hills of Babylon.
Where his body was crowned with the bullets of his brothers.
But when they checked his ID.
They were shocked.
The shooter, the driver, and the masked men saw,
The name on it was Iraqi!!
Neither Shiite nor Sunni.
Neither Kurd nor Turkman.
My country was once Iraq and the ID was Iraqi…

Under the Qurna'a Bridge

When the Euphrates and the Tigris once met.
Shat AL-Arab was born.
In the South,
The fish, the marshes, and the boats emerged every day.
The birds flew on the shore of Shat AL-Arab.
Because of its flows and ebbs.
The land, the trees, the farms were all,
Blossoming, and flourishing.
And they all raced the river's ebbs.
And the fishers sang the anthem of no dry sky.
The fishers went to the depth,
Found the water was mixed with oil.
They found the water brought wealth, fish, and prosperity.
But that was when the rivers married once upon a time.
But later when the rain bled.
And bliss fled far away.
All the boats turned into ghosts,
That rode the back of the night, carrying bullets and bombs,
That became the seeds for our land,
Where the trees were no more trees.
They turned into trunks and merely weeds.
Bullets as seeds!
Trees as weeds!
The people across the Qurna'a Bridge,
Beheld the scene.
When the surface of the Tigris and the Euphrates,
Flowed dimly into Basra.
Bringing the legs of a man from Kadhumyia.
And a head of a child from Adhamyia.
And the veil of a woman from Qadisiya.
And a hand of soldier from Nasyria.
At that moment I believed that,
The Tigris and Euphrates marriage was over,
When all these organs united.
They began to call Iraq, Iraq, and Iraq.
We are Iraq,

We are the land, the rivers and the hearts.
We are the ancient history of the past.
We are the builders of Babylon.
We are the ancestors of Ashurbanipal, Nebuchadnezzar, and Al-Mansur.
We are the now and the present.
Didn't we who invent the first letter on that planet?
Didn't we who issue the first law on that earth?
Where are the writers, thinkers and the literate?
Where are the lawyers and the judges?
In this bleeding red river all lie.
Some of them in their dresses of work.
Others with their pens in their hands.
And my teacher with his books in hand.
And that writer with his poem and the letters on his lips.
That soldiers with his call 'long live Iraq'.
And that child hugging her doll.
And that young student with drilled eyes and heart.
And here is also only a trunk with no hands or legs.
For it trod on a side pavement bomb.
Here is a veil of a woman, but no woman.
Here is the head of a writer who spoke a little loudly in front of the leader.
And that is the arm of a soldier who missed the target on the fronts of Kuwait and
    Iran.
Here is the tongue of a poet who rallied in his dreams against the rule and the rulers.
Here are the legs of a man who marched once to the holy shrine of Hussein.
Oh, Iraq. Is that enough?
When those legs, the heads, the hands meet under that bridge,
And call in the language of the Sumerians and that of Ashur,
They call at night, morning, and at dawn.
No answer is there and no voice coming out of the water.

The Moon

Once I looked at the moon.
The time was 2006.
The land was Iraq.
I was one of the dead,
Marching at dusk,
Searching for absent faces.
I sat on the brink of the Tigris and saw the light of the moon,
Reflected red on the surface there.
The moon was bleeding,
Drops falling slowly on the river of the city of peace.
I roamed the lanes, streets, and lands of the country.
I searched in the atoms of air.
I looked in the pages of night.
In a school I found the ghosts of children playing hide and seek.
They ran and hid, but I saw them.
Running to the side of the cemetery.
And there they laughed, looking at me and laughing.
"We live here, we are sown here".
And we are these weeds that you saw everywhere.
We are the voices of the dead that roam the land at night.
We are the calls to prayers you heard in the morning coming from the minaret.
We are the bomb explosion huggers at 9 am in our class.
We are the cold breeze that touched your skin while you fought.
We are the Shiite and the Sunni you once kicked and then stabbed.
Do you remember?
We are the guards of death in the mosques and churches gates.
They led me by the hand and showed me more.
I beheld their bags torn into pieces.
Their faces were stuck on the glass windows.
Their hands, holding their pencils tightly, were planted on the roofs of classes.
I searched for their mouths and searched and searched.
They looked at me and said:
We are here because of our mouths.
Do not look for them.
They turned toothless because they spoke once of life.
They are here now because once they prayed in the assembly in class.

They are here because they once twittered the song of peace on the surface of the
    Tigris.
They are here to listen to the sounds of their bullets.
To the sounds of their bombs.
That tear, tore, and are tearing our organs every night and day.
We listen to the minarets calling peace and peace, but no hearers.
To the sounds of sermons penetrating the cross in churches.
To the cries of our bemoaned mothers calling for us every night.
To the sigh of our fathers who search for our address in the tombstones.
At that moment, I remembered that I was looking at the surface,
Of the Tigris and saw the bleeding faces reflected there.
And I remembered when they led me to the cemetery.
But I woke up to find that I was inside my heart.
And all these tombs, bullets, and legs and arms were there.
And I was searching inside it for a slaughtered country,
Called Iraq, called Iraq, called Iraq.
I imagined its face was reflected both on the surface of the moon,
And also on the surface of the Tigris.

Cuneiform

Seven thousand years ago,
My country had the oldest written language.
But in the wake of 2003,
My country had a new language,
A language of bullets and fire.
Where the means for saying something was only the Kalashnikov,
Where blood became the letter.
And the gun powder the dots.
A country whose identity is bombing itself day after day,
Where the rain stopped falling on the dales of Babylon.
Iraq is where the masks are worn.
And truths are torn.
Iraq where politics means to have, to take and to leave you at risk.
In Iraq we talk only of the dead.
In Iraq we tread only on the chains of tanks and the triggers.
We tread on the deformed and cut organs of our babies who are badly fed.
In Iraq, oh Iraq.
You look at the sky and see only the smoke of explosions flying over heads.
You see human organs befriend the clouds and hug the angels,
Laugh and then fall on the soldiers' red hackles,
Laugh and then fall on the stars and stripes.
In Iraq where the babies suck the drops of chaos,
Where they feed from the rivers of anguish.
Iraq where the hands know only the touch of wasted life.
And the inhaling of the dry violent air.
Iraq forgot its cuneiform and moulded a new bullet-form.
Where the arrows of death are the new signs of life.
They are the day after day smashing of bodies on the sides of Baghdad.
They are the everyday cries of newly born agonies in the heart of our towns.
Cuneiform is deleted from Iraq's daily life.
Hands, legs and tongues replaced the signs of that old language.
In childhood, children acquire language.
From birth we learn the language of bullets and bombing.

Hammurabi

I am Hammurabi your law father.
I am the law publisher.
I am the peace settler.
I am the fear eraser.
I am the country's new law investigator.
I am your forgotten law father.
I am whose codes are thrown on the shores of the Tigris and the Euphrates.
I am whose codes are dipped in blood.
I am whose codes sunk in 2003 in Shat al-Arab.
Where are the laws now?
I searched in the faces of people,
Day and night,
Morning and evening,
Running and walking,
But no codes were there.
I found remains of them on the drops of blood stuck on the walls of mosques and
churches.
I discovered them in the heads of Shiite and Sunni men lay in the boots of cars late
at night.
I saw them thrown on the pavements of Al-Mutanaby Street with the books and hands
and legs separate.
I saw them laugh at me while travelling on the wings of shot doves in the sky of Iraq.
I saw them in my nightmares when the sky rains bullets and fire.
I searched in the roofs of courts where worms ate the scales of justice morning and
night.
I searched and searched in the streets of Basra,
Where I saw no people, but only ghosts roaming the nights of the dead.
I searched in the cradles of babies.
I searched in the minarets of mosques,
Where shadows of voices clang to the unknown future of Iraq.
I searched the water in the Tigris and found waves of daggers roaming the surface.
Boats of death went carrying corpses of my codes,
And come bringing shadows of nightmarish bombs and bullets and guns.

Mesopotamia

I am Mesopotamia.
The land between the two rivers.
In modern times I am Iraq.
A cradle of civilizations, oh, I was.
A fertile spot of trees, fish, dates, and oil.
My fate is both the oil and the rulers.
My people always sing the anthem of death.
My people always touch the white and turn it into red and dark.
For them, the sword is language.
For them, the word is bullet.
No language in the universe is similar to ours.
In me, there lay men as Ali, Hussein, Abass, and Mohamed.
Their graves turned my soil into sacred shrine,
Their sacrifice whitened my face.
In ancient times, they defended life, God, and man.
In recent times, I became a story, a repetitive story for all other
civilizations.
Just now you may call me a land of stories.
In modern times, in Mesopotamia, there appeared a leader.
He licked my rivers and they became blood in his tongue.
He looked at the roads, clean, crowded, but nodded unsatisfied.
He looked at us, and saw the pens, the hammers, the scissors,
Computers, machines, factories, schools and farms and trees.
This upset him to the end,
He wished his name engraved on the surface of the moon,
On the atoms of air,
In the depth of the oceans, on gold, on streets corners,
On the red coffins of our soldiers in Iran,
In Kuwait, in Khafji, and Mahran,
On the screens of our TVs,
On the pages of children's school books,
And more and more, he forced his name in our mind and heart.
He listened to one ultimate voice and enjoyed it, his voice.
He heard only one sound, the sound of Kalashnikovs.
And he narrated that single story, the story of the dead.
He did and did.

And these streets, these crowds, these pens and farms, and rivers,
All in all, in his hands they became the fall, the rubble, and the darkness of the night.
He loved the guns, the tanks and grenades.
In childhood, he played with only one friend, his own shadow.
Years, and years and years of childhood,
Then he met his mate the devil.
Then they shared the goal.
Just now you may call me a land of stories.

2

A river of mine, forlorn as the rain
I want to run in the dark
Gripping my fists tight
Carrying the longing of a whole year
In each finger, like someone bringing you
Gifts of wheat and flowers

Badr Shakir Al-Sayyab

Phrat

My name is Phrat, now Euphrates, but I preferred the ancient name.
My birth was in Taurus.
The land of falls, and water, and cold.
I passed by the borders in my way to Mesopotamia,
And from there I was pregnant with faces riding my surface at night.
I call them brothers.
They silenced me.
They put the daggers in my side.
I cried and cried and cried, but no help.
I carried them to Ramadi, Fallujah and to Kufa.
And there they bid me farewell.
In them I smelled gunpowder.
And when the waves were high.
I heard a rattling of bullets under the baggage.
They smiled and said hush.
This is for the White house guys.
This is for the red hackled buddies.
This is to keep you safe from them.
They are dark and the axis of evil.
This is for your people, the Sumerians who invented the letter.
The bullet replaced the letter.
Oh, we think better.
For the Babylonians, to save their arts, architecture, and the Babylonian lion.
A gift from the neighbours.
This is for the cradle of civilizations.
For one reason, the past is the best.
And the present is the nest.

Idigna

This is my name,
Do you accept it or is the Tigris better?
I see the Tigris is the recent bloody name.
I pass by the north of Mesopotamia.
I find the land fertile,
The sky filled with clouds, the water is pure,
The people are Kurds.
I find life, flowers, and furs.
I come to Mansour's city among many cities,
But it is not the city of all cities.
I see on the A'ayma Bridge crowds of visitors, walking in sanctity, in peace, in sacred
    breaths,
Marching, reciting verses along the way to Musa AL-kadhum.
Suddenly, oh, a bomb, oh, a bomb
And the crowd disperse,
Some throw and give me their souls freely,
I hug them in my lap,
Some cry loudly in horror.
And some children are laid in my depth laughing slowly, slowly, and slowly.
I see old, old people shout, oh God,
The verses scatter in the air, on my surface,
And while they fell and fell in my depth, they recited the song of life
On the brink of death, I welcome them all
But there is no bomb,
It is on purpose.

Shinar

Have you ever known me?
Have you tried to read my records?
Once upon a time,
I was a cradle for writing in your world.
Once upon a time, I was a place of teaching people how to live together.
A place where people ate together.
A place where people planted and sowed together.
The land was the teacher of man.
The land was the mother of man.
The land was Shinar.
The place where we lived in peace,
Where we shared the letters, dots and signs.
In Shinar the world knew how to plant the seeds of life.
In Shinar the sheep, goat, and ox shared pain and relief.
They ate with us.
Working in prosperity and bliss.
We produced crops that connected us together.
But Shinar now is planted with bombs and is covered by the smoke of death.
Shinar today is the place of burying the living in the caves of darkness.
Shinar today is the cemetery of the ghosts,
Which roam the land day and night.
Today, we plant the seeds of gun powder to kill each other,
To make our organs disperse in Baghdad's corners.
We fight.
We bite.
And we also create fear.
Shinar, the place of green is now the spot of no light.
We look at each other and find only shadows of ghosts,
That carry the daggers of the night,
That smear the faces, the cut legs, hands and fingers of the infants.
We no longer see the water of life running through our veins again.
We never see again the growth of light in our hearts.
We search for ourselves in the dooms of ages and find the ruins appear.
Our hearts throb agonies, pain.
Shinar is the place of rotten corpses roaming the dark souls of the night.
Shinar is the spot of stabbing the infants in the cradles of the future.

Shinar is the birthplace once upon a time of writing.
Now it is the birthplace of writing the names of the dead on the pages of the mornings.
The names of the missed on the covers of boys' school copybooks.
Shinar is the inscriber of the names of the children on the obituary journal.
The hanger of our skeletons on the trees' leaves.
The cut faces of the kidnapped on the rails of stations late at dawn.
We search for the truth that is lost once upon a time.
That we are the originators of writing on the face of the ages,
On the pages of history.
That we are the dreams now of the dawn that is stolen.
But we dreamed for too long and waited and waited,
Till the trees leaned down on the backbones of the hung men.
But the morning no longer prevails.
And the light far away slips.
And the rain rushes arrows of heat,
On our heads that are cut by the fingers of our brothers,
In the boots of their cars,
On the brinks of the Tigris,
On the sides of Shat Al-Arab,
Near the Sayyab statute where the bleeding verses of pain die slowly.
Where the call for Shinar reiterates in the air of the dead rhymes.
Where are the sheep, goat, and ox?
Where is the land?
Where is the word we inherited from Shinar?
We see only the demons that fly around our necks every day.
We see only the gates of bombs widely open in our roads.
Where are the wheat and the barley?
Where are the sheep and the cattle?
Our sheep are the people now!
Our meal is the bullets now!
Oh, come again Shinar.
Oh, come again Shinar.

Tummy

Inside you, oh, tummy I am alive.
I move, I do not freeze.
I eat.
I breathe freely.
Inside you, I feel the breeze of your breath.
I have no boundaries, and no check points, inside you.
I sail like in a boat to nowhere.
I have no marching soldiers drinking verses of martyrdom in cups of icy tanks.
Soldiers who swear the living, the dead and those inside the tummies of Abu Ghraib.
No people praying only when hearing the bombs' sounds coddle their days and nights.
Outside you,
I hear that it is unsafe, insecure and fatal.
Inside I move freely.
They tell me to still be there.
Coming is dangerous.
Inside I move freely.
I listen to bombs, to cries, to sirens.
Inside you, it is different.
Could I go and step outside you?
May I move freely outside you?
Are there graves, shouts and darkness outside you?
Are there red flags outside you, oh tummy?
Are there beauties, mercy and love outside you?
Oh, Iraq, oh, Iraq!
How can I live in you, on your soil without ID card?
Could I call myself a martyr or a victim inside you, oh Iraq?
Could I say Allah Akbar inside you?
Are there two flowing rivers inside you?
Or they are blood-stricken from Baghdad to Basra!
How many floating innocent bodies are there on your surface, oh, Tigris?
I count the days to see you, to touch your cold water, oh Tigris!
Do you flow on both brinks: karkh and Rusafa, oh Tigris?
Have you hugged the floating kids on your surface falling from
Al-A'ayma Bridge, oh Tigris?
Have you spilt any tear for them?
Have you mourned their death?

Have you made their death a ceremony of life or of death?
I beseech you, oh Tigris to talk to me?
Tell me of your pains.
Is Iraq the same or altered by people?
Is there still Allah Akbar announcing our mortality and His immortality?
Are there still mosques to pray in or boots tread on their carpets?
Or there are only the sounds of bombs, bullets and Kalashnikovs?
There is peace, or the illusion is only in my memory and mind?
Is there a bird twittering on your banks the song of paradise lost?
Is AL-Mansur still gazing at his city through the dust of tanks?
Are there on your sides children playing, shouting, and having fun?
Are there voices of kids and babes singing the song of birth?
I yearn, I long for seeing you, but not in darkness.
I see you in my nightmares.
I see you in my walks on the rivers of the nights.
I see your face dusty, gloomy and red.
I see that you have no organs left.
You no longer have any flag.
You have no hands of writers.
Their pens are assassinated inside the car boots.
Your writers do not scribble on papers.
For your papers are webs of the unknown.
Your ideas, oh, writers never heal its pain,
Never bring back its dead young youths that stuck in the fronts of Iran, Kuwait, and
    Saudi Arabia.
Silent, silent you are, oh Sheiks and priests!
Say, call, preach.
Do not you breathe its breeze every day?
Is there no word to utter for us?
Why you are only long beards, big turbans, and big mouths.
You relish our blood spilt on the pavements every day.
In your late night enthusiasm when wrestling with your lies.
In your sticky chairs in the parliament.
I see you clean and our children drag their filth with the inhales of disgrace in Abu
    Ghraib.
I see you laugh when our mothers sip the dirt of our neighbours' favours!!
I see your cars shining when my face in the tummy is deformed by the tanks' and
    aircrafts' uranium . . .

I look at myself in the tummy and find no Iraqi,
But a memory of a nightmare that haunts my soul.
Later I remember that this is my birth dream as an Iraqi baby.
On the surfaces of the Tigris and the Euphrates.
In the palms of my father's hands that were eaten by the war on terror.
In the side of the Mosques in which corpses of Sunni and Shiite get married in the
    ceremony of sect fight.
Sect fight calls from the doors of graves:
Kill your brothers, suck their bloods, destroy their homes, cut their organs, and haunt
    their wives and kids in the name of democracy and freedom.
In the sound of Big Ben's declaring the dawn of freedom of action for every human.
I see that my birth is better to stay an enigma unsolved and hung dangling in the door
    of time.
I sense no soul throbbing in my chest, but only I feel pictures of flowing ruin.
Pictures of my hand cut and thrown in front of the red hackle in the tank.
I smell that picture inside me of the street of Mutanaby crowded with piles of roasted
    corpses that cry:
Long live the leader, the hackles and stripes!
I see dots of holes inside my chest flowing dead wishes mixed with gun powders.
I try to flee from my chest,
But to nowhere, there is only one way out:
Iraq, Iraq, Iraq.
Your south is oozing oil, but drinks filth.
Your south becomes a nightmare of marching armies at night.
Why your south is no longer the voice of poetry.
No longer hearing Sayaab's rhymes sung by the people.
No longer the sounds from the minaret penetrating our hearts.
The south, oh, my country, is a dead story told by an exhausted soldier coming from
    war.
The south in my country is the pool of bullets ringing our skulls every day and night.
The south is the soul taker.
In it, we hear every morning only the twittering of the dead.
Our dead corpses' ghosts roam our memories moment after moment.
The south, oh the south.
It is no longer the anchor of ships.
I see it loaded with weapons of mass non-existence,
The regeneration and birth of boys to die for a case unborn yet.
I see the south as the ogre that eats my mother's breast, mouth and gentle fingers.

That devours my father's nails, manhood and throat.
No man is left in the south except skeletons of voices,
That dream of the death of the leader and the obituary of terror.
The resurrection of death.
I look at the trees and see only the shadows of corpses following me.
They laugh and dance on the coffins brought by the bullets.
They track every single tummy and stab it.
For fear of giving birth to life still to come in illusions.
I weep and weep, but I see no tears.
I have hollow holes under my eyebrows, no eyes are left.
Iraq, oh.
The dry river of worms that creep quickly and eat me in the tummy…
Please, leave me in the tummy.
In the tummy.

Oh, My Father

In the dawn of terror.
In 2005.
On the shore of the Tigris.
I saw his face reflected on the window glass,
Looking at my face in awe.
Wanting to talk, but the tongue uprooted was,
By the fingers of a brother, who long ago ate with him,
Sat with him, played in childhood with him.
The fingers of a man called opposite sect.
The dagger of a man, who polished it on my father's neck.
I saw his eyes on my window crying sighs and pains.
His eyes were merely holes and no eyes.
They dug them out.
His nostrils were two big empty bullets.
His mouth was a hollow deserted cave.
Where the agonies of the past lay warmly.
His face vanished suddenly and I followed.
I searched for my father's face in the nearby orchard.
I saw only the tombstones of the dead.
Tombstones taken from the bricks of the rubble of the mosques and churches.
The dead Shiite and the dead Sunni.
I read and read.
The names were inscribed by the bullets of the tanks.
By the sidewalk bombs.
That devoured the souls of the children on their way to school.
The names were painted by the blood of the infants in the cradles of death.
The names were you and me and you and me.
And there, no wreaths were laid.
And there only the smell of the oil of the tanks dominated.
And there I saw the hackles of the Scottish soldiers fly highly.
I saw the stripes of the superpower flag delete the infants' dates of birth.
I called loudly, oh father!
No tomb was there for you, oh father.
No name was there for you, oh father.
These names were not your name.
No memory was left.

Where are your face and body?
No legs, hands or head are there for you, oh father.
Where is your smile that filled my days with future?
Where are the fingers that touched my youth tenderly?
I see the ghosts of terror fly above my head, oh father.
I see the shooting of the tanks surrounding me, oh father.
I smell the gun powder pervades the sky.
I tread on corpses…
I look and see just war and war.
Where is your history, oh, my father?
Where are your pens and papers and ink?
I see them all float on the brink of the Tigris.
I see them all coated with blood.
I see them and I see no letters.
They turned into an event in the war on terror.
And the war on man.
And the war on the Tigris and the dead.
I see your history is buried there.
Then his face appears and says:
Hold on my son.
Just one day you come and join us.
One day you will be on the queue.
One day when the chain of the tank revolves round your neck.
The stripes of the superpower flag turn arrows into your body.
When the red hackles of the beret penetrates your heart.
When the bombs of the F35 fighter cut your tongue and throat.
And the smoke of the burning oil from Kuwait chokes you.
At that time, you happily join my face.
At that moment you believe that man is rubble.
That man is uranium's depleted son.
That man has no longer any history.
A being with no voice.
A being with claws that scratch the souls of the dead.
That man is a bullet idol residing in the memory of the dead.
That we will no longer deserve being called Iraqis.
At that time only I sensed suddenly,
Something treads on my cut head.
It was the boot of the soldier waking me up from the prison of freedom nightmare.

Doors

For us many doors are there.
From which we have no way out.
We try to look, but see no outlets.
The steps are taboos.
The keys are hollow skulls.
The holes in the doors are starts for repressed fires,
Where no one dares look through.
Illusions are they and we keep silencing our wishes,
Forgetting the dreams of outlets,
Of going out of the wombs of pain and torture.
Our sighs kill the sights of dreaming nights in our heads.
We try to look through these doors uselessly.
To the dead mornings that are absent from our blurred eyes.
To the bleeding nights that dominate our corners.
To the streets, stars, and the descending moon.
But no glimpse of them was apparent,
On the surface of the Tigris,
On the sides of the Euphrates,
On the gates of Baghdad or the rivers' water.
We look and look through these doors.
We imagine seeing the sun rising in the heavenly sky.
The legs, the heads, the fingers hung there by the deadly waves of blood.
The wind of the present sweeps our memories.
The doors are unlocked, but we see them like ghosts that terrify us.
That imprison our souls in the wild country of our body.
The infants of our country beg for life from the hands of the shooters.
From the boots of the kidnapping cars.
From the high wind of our reveries.
From the door steps of our leaders,
Who ignored the rotten loafs surrounding our lips day and night.
We smell from the inside of these doors the wet tears of our dead forefathers.
To our lungs, these doors welcome the bullets of the marching tanks of the superpower
    soldiers.
These doors push us inside the wombs of forgetfulness and loss.
To the unknown present that is looming with bombs waiting for our souls to reap.
These doors are open, but locked on our souls forever.

Tears

Oh, children of Mesopotamia.
On the surfaces of your cheeks,
I saw drops of flowing tears.
The smell of their nostalgic wishes emitted from their repressed voices.
And the doleful cries of their mouths are kept unheard.
I sensed their hearts were rivers of pain.
The future of their present was blurred by the smoke of loss.
The everyday life of their record was assassinated on the brink of the Tigris.
These children were born in the laps of wrong.
They fed from the chest of anguish.
And given bread by the hands carrying whips.
Speaking the language of bombs and explosions.
These hands were covered by the children's blood.
By the dead dreams of their nights.
These hands were givers of darkness and bloody floods.
They looked at us and saw the wealth of absence pervading Iraq.
They dreamed of golden chairs, leaden cups, and unfinished riches.
They paved our dreams with nails of fire.
They painted our bags with asphalt.
Their voices diffused nonsense and chaos.
Children of Mesopotamia we are!
Of law and the two rivers.
Of the first born letter on that earth.
Of Babylon's hanging gardens.
We were born surrounded by the chains of your tanks and the leader's whips.
We slept on the cradles of fear.
And awoke by the kicks of the soldiers on Basra borders.
We are the carriers of your guilt and sins.

3

They did not recognize me in the shadows
That suck away my color in this Passport
And to them my wound was an exhibit
For a tourist who loves to collect photographs
They did not recognize me.

Mahmoud Darwish

One after one

In the dawn of history,
Our mothers delivered us on the shores of two flowing rivers.
The light of hope nurtured our dreams of glowing future.
We saw only days and sunrises.
On the sides of Baghdad, Shiites and Sunnis shook hands.
In Rusafa and Karkh, we built our first arch of heritage.
In the two sides, the air was blowing equally on our farms.
The nights were far away from our sights.
The moon was our Scheherazade who told us of our glory.
And the stars emanated the fragrance of our soul's victory.
Never greedy we were!
But dreamed only of peace.
And once upon a time.
On the eve of war.
The great war on terror!!
When that dream eclipsed all of a sudden.
We turned into warriors of the night.
The reflection of the moon rained bullets instead of incense.
And the glimpse of hope was kidnapped at the gate of Ishtar.
The birds of light left their nests,
Fleeing to a drowned past of Iraq,
Searching the maps of unknown lands,
Searching the pages of lost times.
These birds at last forsook their mission.
And to the ecliptic moon of Mesopotamia they led their way.
War after war.
Ruler after another.
And we, the children of the two rivers lived in gloom,
For the lethal circle of the leaders on our heads.
When at last the war on terror invaded our hearts.
Breaking our ribs,
And treading on our faces and with uranium choked our lungs.
When the bombs smashed our mosques,
And the churches,
And kidnapped our loaf.
The roads of peace became caves of terror.

And the laps of tender turned into ovens of horror.
War after war.
And leader after leader.
And Iraq is the port of travel.
It is the gate of expatriation.
And its people are the launchers of immigration.
To its assassinated youth of peace, Iraq fled.
Iraqis addicted to agony and desertion.
Once upon a time,
We were born on the brinks of the two flowing rivers.
On the eve of history.
We awoke and found a bomb and a tank.
On the dawn of our life, we saw the Tigris and the Euphrates.
Both ablated by the blast.
And the echoes of our aspirations,
Deleted from the world's maps.   .
Once upon a time,
We were delivered on the two rivers' sides.

Pencils

I searched the lanes of our land.
I roamed the farms of the country.
I wanted to find the people who were once people of the land of the Tigris.
I found the Tigris tears wetting the land.
The grass of the orchards was mixed with the powder of the guns.
The people planted flower seeds in the wake of dawn.
Our people watered the land from the river of Shat Al-Arab,
Where the boats of hopes were reflected on the land's image.
But time comes when,
The school classes chaotically hug each other in fire.
They embraced in destruction under the bomb's lust.
I searched for the bags, the pencils and the flags.
I searched for your children's names on the bloody scraps of exploded cars.
I searched for their presence on the walls of burned houses.
On the smoke of the burning wells in Kuwait,
On the buried whips of our torturers underground.
I searched for their voices in the mouths of the opened graves in Iraq.
I once imagined there were faces, eyes and arms.
That laughed, looked and shook hands.
That once played in the play-ground under the light of the moon.
That once wrote the name of Iraq on the pages of the day.
On the surface of the Tigris and on the moving waves of their dreams.
Faces that are now roasted.
Hands that are now ousted.
And tongues that are now obliterated.
And eyes that draw castles in the air of Iraq.
Still searching for their pencils to draw the map of life,
On the borders of blood.
Still searching the streets for the pencils that will shape the new garden, for the dead
    and the car-booted legs, arms and hands.
Still searching the caskets for a memory of return,
Of verses to be recited on the minaret of mercy,
Of quite sermons delivered on the nails of the bleeding cross.
Of our prayers that are forgotten once in the desert storm.
I searched in the old people's silence in the queue for death.

Searching for our rhymes that are sacrificed on the edges of the guns.
I live searching.
I will die searching.
For a country that roams my depleted presence.
Searching...

A Book

In the book of history I looked for a country.
That once was a country.
A country whose people are turned into living ghosts.
Whose pens are arrows of illusions.
A country that knew fertility once upon a time.
And built Babylon by the water of the two rivers.
A country that becomes a story and a song.
A story for the nations.
A story of sweeping caskets roaming its lanes,
Every night and day.
A story of the faces deformed by the aircrafts.
Of the men who are tired of dreaming of meeting and departure.
By the stars, the stripes and the red hackles.
A story that is told by an innocent.
Whose mouth is blocked by bullets.
Whose voice is repressed by the wind of the desert storm.
Whose image is deleted by the marching tanks.
It once had a sky.
It once had a language.
It once had a name and a flag.
I searched in the book and searched.
I found the lanes are crowded by marching souls,
That led their way to the cemetery of the night.
I followed the dead voices lurking in the graves.
I tried to make them utter, speak, and say something.
To see what had happened, what happen and what will happen to us.
I smelled the fragrance of quietness covering their cries under the tombs.
But the tanks' sounds trod on the leaves of the trees.
And reaped the farms of life.
Uprooted the infants from the cradles of hope.
A country whose leader painted his image near the dreams edges.
A leader who painted the morning with the claws of doom.
Who dreamt of weapons, skulls and skeletons.
Who booked cemeteries for the coming generations.
Who built refuges and released the souls out of their cages.
A leader dreamt of riveting his name on the surface of blood.

On the echoes of spaceships sounds.
On the foreheads of the dead soldiers in Kuwait and Khafji.
On the atoms of the air pervading Abu-Ghraib and Bukka.
On the people's certificates of death.
On the twittering sounds of the migrating birds from the south.
On the faces, on the hands, on the names of infants yet unborn.
He inscribed the letters of the nations' names on the tombstones of history.
I searched the book and found the medal that the leader dreamt of.
It was a tank with stars, stripes and hackles on top.
It was an aircraft with depleted arms at rear.
It was a shore of chaos, pain, shame, and fear.
The leader's medal was f 35 for his people to hug.
It was a shower of bullets to kill us for we are the bugs.
It was the present gift of freedom coated lies.
It was merely the voices of crying tortured infants in cradles.
It was the assassination of a Shiite in a car boot.
It was the killing of a Sunni on the brink of the Tigris.
It was the bloody shouts of exploded cars in Al-Mutanaby Street.
It was Abu-Ghraib's strangled cut organs of Iraqis,
It was the deformed souls of the generation after generation of Iraq.
It was their ablated tongues hung on its walls.
It was the whips crowning their feeble corpses.
It was the night armies of the borders invading our dreams.
It was the arms loaded boats digging Shat-Al-Arab days and nights.
It was the chains of fear revolving round the mothers' hearts.
Round the men's dreaming heads that were stuck on the street's bloody pavements .
It was the leader who was there.
It was the leader who stayed there.
It was the leader's image painted on the tank's sides.
It was the leader's voice merging with the marching caskets.
It was his touch that formed our loss in time.
I searched the book and found his military smell pervading our lungs and choked
    them forever.
It was him.
It was the book.

Flying Man

In Mustansirya University, I parked.
One by one in the early morning students alighted.
And I was there for a while.
And when I said good-bye,
I saw a flying smoky body,
Without legs.
Mounting the flag post in the centre of the university.
I held the stern tightly,
For fear of meeting him there.
I smoked roasted bodies' on the pavement,
Crying for death not life.
From the middle of all that side pavement explosion
I beheld the flying body seizing a pen in one finger,
And in the other a bleeding paper,
I saw his deformed face,
That was handsome once upon a time,
Tortured by exhaustion.
He gazed at the others who were with him.
Those who joined his death party.
They were turned into roasted corpses,
With no organs,
Only, smoke, dust and ashes.
They were once students there.
But now,
Lay with no voices here.
All I remembered was the flying man,
Who was once one of them in the car with me,
But turned upside down in the air,
And his body was flamed with fear,
And when he fell, I sighed.
He met the others on the pavement,
Lying there.
I called aloud:
Where are the students and the pens?
Where are the white shirts and grey skirts,
Worn out now by the bloody winds of the bad.

And the smiles were assassinated in the dens.
Where terror put his plans,
To turn us into tombstones,
Where prayers never recited on our souls.
Where all of us dead and life became a cave of horrors.
Once in Mustansirya University, I parked.

Nostalgia

And now, how you are there and I am here?
Man turns an abyss resident.
The birds are no longer twittering lyrics of life.
Too long is the road to the future, but you, living in memory and mind.
How now I see the moon descends,
Clouds group to cover aches and they nurture.
My pen is broken by the marching tanks,
On the sides of the Tigris,
Where we once twittered our unrealised dreams aloud and aloud.
How now we parted,
By the rhymes of bullets that haunt our sleepless nights.
Stay there for it is better,
Stay there for it is safer,
Stay away from me and the burning land.
Stay awake for Iraq is looping inside its caves again.
Stay there for Iraqis are used to smell the stink of the ablated organs,
That are cut and thrown in the boots of cars early at dawn,
That are given as gifts to the herbs of the Tigris and the Euphrates
But do not wait for me,
For I sink now in the bleeding rivers of the past.
I live on the shores of oozing pains.
I am reciting every morning your hymns of loss and departure,
Remembering the echoes of our wishes on the surface of the water,
That bleeds sighs, pain and death.

Birth

Where life seems mess,
Man turns into an abyss.
Where hearts leave faith,
Friends and sweethearts are meaningless.
And you, who was near,
Now in nostalgia drowns,
To be meaningful and serene.
And you who backed me in the past,
Turned into a shooter today,
Hiding in the jungles of the night,
Wearing the masks of the ghosts,
Which roam the mountains' sides.
Searching for me to snipe at dawn.
Looking at the bleeding faces of the lanes,
Digging the orchards of the dead,
Writing rhymes of loss,
Inscribing our organs on the sleepy drops of the bloody Tigris.
But you will find our names,
Recited on the destroyed minarets and the deserted churches,
Mentioned only on the pages of false and fake histories.
Our names that are roaming the night cemeteries of Iraq.
Our names that are floating on the water of the retreating Euphrates,
Our names that are sunken in the birth of chaos.

Waiting

Waiting on the steps of the future for too long,
We paved our nights with fake dreams.
Where the new comers appear as ghosts of horror,
Which roam our present and spread fear.
What would happen then?
If people rise ...
The turmoil is on the brink.
We live in woods,
The land weeps blood.
It agonised for long.
It waited them for long!
They failed.
Revenge is the scene,
Where our days are stepped on by the tanks' marching chains.
And the air is filled with echoes of the dead cries.
Only organs of kids, old women and men lay in the markets
And the sirens of death invaded our dawns.
The past was merciless, bleeding, screaming.
We became the past!!
We are turned into incarnate images of lost memories.
The land no longer waited our steps.
The air leaves our space for the smoky burning sky near Kuwait.
The borders are pregnant with the buried organs of our dead soldiers in Al-Khafji.
We waited for you for long.
Your new voices saddened the dreams of the young in schools.
Waiting is a nightmare revolving round our necks at night.
Waiting is a start for a new call of:
"Short live the leaders" ...
"Long live the dead dreams" ...

4

New Year, don't come to our homes, for we are wanderers
From a ghost-world, denied by man.
Night flees from us, fate has deserted us
We live as wandering spirits
With no memory
No dreams, no longings, no hopes.

Nazik Al-Malaika

Idigna Revisited

Once upon a time, I once sat beside Idigna,
A river where the trees hugged the twittering birds.
By its sides, I grew up day after day,
And listened to the fragrant echoes of the waves' rhyming roaring.
But when the 2003 tanks deleted the grass that paved Idigna's two sides,
My verses cried for resurrection from death.
I saw how the birds forsook the nests,
The murmurings ebbs and flows were filled with blood,
At that time only, my verse started to revive,
The lines became arrows of anger that survive,
The tanks, aircrafts, and bullets' echoing sounds
I wrote to Idigna a poem of pain and torture,
I declared to the world that our river
Is turned into a living casket,
Where human organs shouted for freedom,
Where tongues of babies were tied to the cross,
Where my rhymes feared to be uttered by the river's side,
Then I understood that Idigna was my soul's inspiration

Dream

In the dawn of 2003, I dreamt of Idigna,
Shrouded by mystery and covered by doom.
Its brinks appeared spotted with chains of tanks,
Where the birds, the swans and doves forsook their resorts of bloom.
The boats flooded with travellers of the nights,
Whose baggage, only for bullets, has a room.
Their voices are whispers of revenge,
Their masks are deformed by their bombs,
And the light of the sky turned into dead shadows.
Idigna carried them to the city of peace,
Which became a spot of legs, hands, and cut throats.
It mourned the flows and ebbs that are gone with no trace,
It cried for all the lovers' lively steps on its shore,
For their defeated aspirations and promises.
The light the city of peace reflected in the past,
Became shreds of darkness covering the first flow,
And the ebb that was the last.
Idigna, Wake up to life,
Clean your shores of bullets and bombs.

Cities

Do not laugh and do not be appalled
When you see that the dead invade our cities.
Darkness is their tool.
And light recedes in front of them.
Our cities...
Where waves of blood rush on doorsteps.
Where sounds of tanks' chains occupy our dreams at night.
And the cries of tortured people are kept out of the sight.
Their pains are torches that light
The way to the gates of cemeteries.
The leaders' calls of freedom, democracy and lies-coated peace,
Are all drowned with the wishes of the young in the Euphrates.
The dead who roam our cities have no faces,
They hold masks in their hands to cover them,
And their voices are heard only in election months
When all our dreams become posters on the walls in streets,
When all our pains are swept away,
And our anguish is buried away,
And they paint our days with flowers,
And draw our morning with touches of peace and no sighs.
These are our cities where the dead are angels of hope,
And the living are reapers of souls.
Come and have a look,
At the schools that turn into cemeteries,
And the holy shrines where bombs welcome their visitors,
And look at the legs, heads and hands
Which were planted in the waves of Idigna and the Euphrates.
The veil of a woman,
And the beret of a soldier,
And the school bag of a child,
Which all with blood soaked..
Come and have a look,
At our churches where the twittering of peace on their gates were assassinated.
And at our mosques where the organs of prayers paint the floors that were tainted.
Our cities are cities of roaming ghosts and tanks...

Insomnia

Pens, poems, and scribbles,
The letters are lost in the memories of no peace.
The poets' fingers are chained by whips.
Their thoughts are pregnant with insomnia.
They never forget their rhymes.
Their imagination lives in silence,
Covered by darkness.
In Iraq,
Every morning it rains blood.
Our sparrows twitter sadness.
And in every market,
Every day, a new pain is born.
And our bodies release their souls with no guilt for free.
Oh, Iraq.
In Mustansirya,
The bombs call our souls from time to time.
Al-Athamyia inhales only death bullets.
In Khadhumyia,
Where the recitation and calling for prayer,
Hug the doors of heaven,
But the minarets' calls are without identity.
The colours of the streets are still red.
And you are Iraq,
Since seven thousand years,
Year after year,
Your blood is flowing.
And you are Iraq,
The wound of the civilizations.
The birthplace of the letter.
The light of the devout.
And you are Iraq,
A revolution against wrong.
And a volcano where the feet of darkness fear to tread.
And you are Iraq,
Whose light is not seen by the envying eyes.
You are the palm trees, high and proud all the time.

You are Idigna and Phrat.
You are the wound and the martyr.
Who was assassinated at the dawn of the war.
I dream of seeing you once again,
In a new light,
When your parts clean the dust of mortars,
And delete all the trenches,
And tread on all the camps,
And stand up again high and proud,
Surrounded by the halo of every church and every mosque,
Where the calls for holiness and purity revive again.
You are Iraq.
You stay Iraq.

Skulls

These skulls, left there underground,
Seek release from the dust of death.
And these bones cry for flesh
That was exploded by gasoline!
The chemical man invented a quick remedy,
For their revolutionary pains,
And injected their wishes with bullets.
And turned their eyes into hollow holes,
Where the future blurred forever.
Their voices, like arrows thrown in the desert air,
No purpose, no aim, and no destination.
Has anybody looked in their diary?
And has he found out that their books,
Pens and papers were burned by wars
Has anybody seen how their prayers,
Were assassinated on the doorsteps of mosques.
Their aspirations to change were trodden on by
The boots of marching soldiers.
There underground, they lay.
Can you recognise who is a Sunni, or a Shiite or a Turkman, or a Kurd?
All grouped together, melted together,
And recited the anthem of resurrection.
One day,
The circle will come back.

Questions

Don't ask me who I am.
Don't check my Id.
For I left a country far behind,
Carrying my memories with me.
A country clouded by the smokes of oil wells,
And pregnant with statutes of the leader.
In every street, we have to bow in front of them,
And polish the leader's image displayed on the corners of our streets,
And on the walls of our schools.
A leader who teaches us the value of silence.
And the wisdom of obedience,
And the happiness of death.
That the war is an honour,
Fought for keeping his speeches forever on TV screens.
Don't check my birthplace.
For I was a man of the city of the marshes,
Where there were only shadows of marshes.
Where the fish was depleted by the Desert Storm bounties.
Where it fed from the bombs of the tanks.
A city of poets where no poets live there,
For the leader erased their rhymes,
By the whips of pain
By blocking the power of feelings inside them.
Don't ask me what my name is,
I am the two rivers,
Babylon,
Shat Al-Arab,
I am the marshes, the riverbanks, and the holy shrines.
This is my passport,
That every immigration officer in the world had seen.
I left my memories on the pages of history for the world to read.
Never ashamed.

Sirens

Sirens, sirens, sirens.
Tanks, tanks, tanks.
All what we hear is sirens.
All what we see is tanks.
The first works hard day and night.,
Bringing our souls to an end of pain,
And sending them to the cemeteries of the unknown
Where all of our organs, mixed with misery,
Lay in bags
With no names on them,
With no memories.
No past to be recalled.
Only the exploded present,
Where the voices of crying babies
And the cries of bereaved mothers
Are silenced by the sirens.
Here, the day mourns the night.
Here, the night mourns the day.
Time becomes a circle of fire,
Revolving around our heads,
Devouring our souls which welcome the sirens.
Sirens, sirens, sirens.
Tanks, tanks, tanks.

Basra

Here you are.
This is my birthplace
Where the tanks roaming our lanes,
Turning our music into clatter.
The chains of tanks delete our memories,
Our facial expressions.
The mortars visit the airport day and night.
The bullets become our newspapers
In which we read our daily condolence.
We forget how to listen to the minarets' calls,
Where the prayers lose all their essence.
This is my city.
Where the churches turn into nests.
The cross cries for the choirs
Mercy is kidnapped by bullets.
This is my birthplace,
Where verses reiterates the cadence of doom.
This is my city where Shat Al-Arab,
Imports boats of bombs,
And exports our bodies,
Cut into parts,
In the boots of cars in the farms of the night.
This is my city,
This is my city.

The war on Idigna

Tanks faced by bullets
Bullets faced by bombs
Bombs faced by legs, heads and hands.
Voices invaded the street.
Screams covered the sky.
The street was filled with slogans,
The first was: "the war on terror".
The second was "the land defender".
The first said: "I am the tyranny eraser".
The second said: "I am the land defender".
The first said "I am the freedom, democracy and peace spreader".
The second cried" I am death that comes to take your soul
Quick and quicker.
The street was filled with slogans.
The street smoked death.
Bombs, bullets.
Bombs, bullets.
Blood and fire.
The voices quietened.
The triggers, tired, exhausted, fell down
On Idigna.
The sounds of the tanks' chains echoed in the sky.
No more slogans were there!
Only drops of blood painting the dawn of 2003.
Only the mothers' cries were heard in the distance.
The twittering of the birds was hugged by the bombs' explosions.
No more songs.
No more slogans.
The country is bullets.
The country is bombs.
The country is hands, legs and heads.
Tanks faced by bullets
Bullets faced by bombs
Bombs faced by legs, heads and hands.

Echo

I walked to the sides of Idigna that once were filled with flowers,
Crying "why?"
Why is this happening to us, oh, my country?"
I uttered the words aloud again and again
To reach the doors of heaven,
To penetrate the cross,
To be riveted on the walls of mosques and churches,
To go inside the mothers' broken hearts,
To break the silence of the cemeteries that devoured our kidnapped corpses,
To the rain that forsook our land for long,
To the ebbs and flows of your two rivers,
To the voices of the choirs,
To the anthem of my country,
To the fronts of wars that were fed up with our bones,
To the deceased wishes of our forefathers,
To the trees where Al-Sayyab sat and wrote his rhymes,
To the hope of peace which vanished with the war on terror.
I walked and uttered and cried,
But no answer was there!
I listened and listened,
Only the echo,
Returns to me,
"Why"?

5

I wrote these verses to you, oh, my country; verses from a lover who is infatuated by you, your heritage and your two rivers

Arrival

I came when stars' lights were reflected on the meadows.
I waited your arrival by the side of the lake,
Glimpsing at your image engraved in my heart.
But would I see you when light might disappear in your presence?
But darkness would show your beauty and brightness.
I waited your appearance covering the grassy orchards.
My breaths leapt in joy when I dreamed of your arrival at that night.
I looked at the grass and the lake water flowing.
I waited till the dawn disclosed the quiet leave of the moon's light.
The day revealed the night's departure in the early morning.
My waiting heart beats felt your image on the lake's water.
I raised my head, seeing the water was disturbed by the birds' flutter.
By the echoing morning breeze rising from the sides of the trees' leaves.
I discovered the morning light hid behind the glimmering mantle of your arrival.

At Dawn

When the moon's light reflects on the flowing water of the lake.
I discover that your love shakes my heart at dawn.
The dewy trees' leaves sense my presence,
And the grassy meadows pave my way to you.
By the side of the lake I smell the fragrance of your arrival.
I sense your light steps tread on my heart's waiting beats,
Come to me in silence and at dawn,
For the night is the mantle of dreams and longing.
And when the stars' glimmering light recedes.
The moon and the meadow and the lake,
With me are all awake.
Waiting for the quiet beats of your advent.
And the night, the morning and my breaths,
Speed to the flowing lake to see,
Your presence reflected on the drops of flowing lake.
I sense that you are a shadow roaming my night.
That you are a secret of the heart,
Revealed to me in the wake of dawn.

Reflection

From the window of the night,
I looked for a sign that once linked me to you.
The moon's light that appeared reflected on the lake,
The stars that hugged the darkness and wrapped it in light,
And the grassy meadows and the dewy leaves hanging on the park's gate,
Are all stops for the secrets of our love,
Are all symbols of a love that was,
And the cold breeze that coddled your honey skin near the lake,
Is now waiting for your arrival at dawn.
The melodious words that once were uttered by you,
Are echoing in my night's longing hours.
Bringing hope to the days that longed for you.
To the running moments of my breaths.
I walked to see your reflection in the lake,
But found the moon's light shrouded by your presence.
And the stars left their space to your gleaming image to nurture.

Meeting

At the sea side where first our hearts met together.
The murmuring waves hugged the breeze surrounding your breaths.
The cooing doves picked your words and sang them to me.
In my hand, the roses hid in shame when facing your beauty.
But your presence covered them with life.
The trees leaves shook to greet your arrival.
I wandered with you for no destination, listening to the voice of love.
The sun dragged its light from your brightness.
And your whispers, as rhymes of eternity, turned me into a bard.
All these steps with you are glimpses of hope incarnate in my heart.
The minutes passed like a trace of light waning from a descending moon.
I looked at the waves, the sun, the doves, and imagined I saw you there.
I searched for you in their shine, their sounds and brightness.
The sea reminded me that, every morning, I lived with your memory on its side.

Notes

Page

11— Red Hackles: the berets of the Scottish regiment soldiers' uniform have red hackles on top of them. It is the regiment that entered Basra, in the South of Iraq in 2003.

11— Stars and Stripes: they refer to the USA flag.

17— Phrat: it is the Greek name for the Euphrates, meaning "fertilizing".

17— The White House Guys: refer to the USA soldiers.

18— Idigna: is the original Sumerian name for the Tigris.

25— The Stripes of the Superpower: refer to the flag of the USA.

38— Bukka: is a prison in Basra in the South of Iraq.

Lightning Source UK Ltd.
Milton Keynes UK
UKOW08f0130130517

301104UK00001B/158/P